W9-BXU-936

ANIMAL CANNIBALS

Bullfrogs

Sam Hesper

PowerKiDS
press.

New York

Published in 2015 by The Rosen Publishing Group, Inc.
29 East 21st Street, New York, NY 10010

First Edition

Editor: Caitie McAneney
Book Design: Michael J. Flynn

Photo Credits: Cover Chris Hill/Shutterstock.com; p. 5 Gary Meszaros/Visuals Unlimited/Getty Images; p. 6 Helen E. Grose/Shutterstock.com; p. 7 EcoPrint/Shutterstock.com; p. 9 Ingrid Curry/Shutterstock.com; p. 11 Ilias Strachinis/Shutterstock.com; p. 12 Nashepard/Shutterstock.com; p. 13 Anthony Mercieca/Science Source/Getty Images; p. 14 katatonia82/Shutterstock.com; p. 15 Photo Researchers/Science Source/Getty Images; p. 17 Jupiterimages/Photos.com/Thinkstock.com; p. 18 Fabio Sacchi/Shutterstock.com; p. 19 (female bullfrog) Michael Richardson/Shutterstock.com; p. 19 (male bullfrog) Bruce MacQueen/Shutterstock.com; p. 21 Dan Suzio/Science Source/Getty Images; p. 22 Michiel de Wit/Shutterstock.com.

Library of Congress Cataloging-in-Publication Data

Hesper, Sam.
 Bullfrogs / Sam Hesper.
    pages cm. — (Animal cannibals)
 Includes index.
 ISBN 978-1-4777-5819-9 (pbk.)
 ISBN 978-1-4777-5821-2 (6 pack)
 ISBN 978-1-4777-5818-2 (library binding)
 1. Bullfrog—Juvenile literature. I. Title.
 QL668.E27H47 2015
 597.8'92—dc23
                                    2014032896

Manufactured in the United States of America

CPSIA Compliance Information: Batch #CW15PK: For Further Information contact Rosen Publishing, New York, New York at 1-800-237-9932

Contents

Bullfrog Bites

Have you ever heard the deep call of a bullfrog at night? They could be looking for a **mate** or out for a nighttime hunt. Bullfrogs may seem harmless to you, but these frogs are fearsome predators in the animal world!

The bullfrog is the largest frog in North America. It can grow up to 8 inches (20 cm) long. American bullfrogs rule the freshwater **habitats** of North America. They have green or brown skin, spots, and wide mouths. These nighttime hunters have large mouths for a reason—they're big eaters. Bullfrogs are known to eat anything they can fit in their mouth. They'll even eat other bullfrogs!

A cannibal is an animal that eats another animal of its own kind. Bullfrogs are some of the most famous animal cannibals!

What Are Bullfrogs?

Bullfrogs are amphibians, which means they live part of their life in water and part on land. Amphibians live in most places around the world that are near freshwater, except Antarctica. Amphibians are vertebrates, which means they have a backbone. They're **cold-blooded**. Nearly 5,000 frog **species** live around the world.

American bullfrog

Bullfrogs fill their lungs with air and make noises that sound like the deep "moos" of bulls. That's how they got their name!

African bullfrog

When most people talk about bullfrogs, they're usually talking about the American bullfrog. They're the most common and wide-ranging bullfrog species. Other large frogs are also called bullfrogs, such as the African bullfrog and Indian bullfrog. This book will focus on the American bullfrog, but other bullfrogs are known to be cannibals, too!

Adapting to New Places

American Bullfrogs are native to the central and eastern United States, southeastern Canada, and northeastern Mexico. However, many American bullfrogs now live outside of their native homes, including areas covering most of North America and several South American countries.

American bullfrogs have spread around the world. They live in many European and Asian countries. People first took bullfrogs across oceans and continents for food. In some countries, frog legs are a special treat! Some bullfrogs escaped from people who brought them to a new place or were set free. These bullfrogs **adapted** to living in their new habitats.

American bullfrogs are good at adapting to new places. They need only food, places to hide, and freshwater to keep their skin moist.

FOOD FOR THOUGHT

American bullfrogs tend to be active in spring, summer, and fall. In winter, they usually hibernate, or go into a deep sleep.

Sight and Sound

Bullfrogs have excellent vision. Their big eyes are on top of their head. This allows them to peek above the water's surface while hiding most of their body underwater. This is how bullfrogs hide from predators and **prey**. Bullfrogs can also feel movement in the water around them.

Bullfrogs have excellent hearing, too. Bullfrogs have a pair of tympana on the outside of their body. Tympana are **membranes** that act as eardrums and protect the inner ears from dirt and water. The tympana are located behind the eyes. Excellent hearing helps bullfrogs find mates and stay safe from predators.

FOOD FOR THOUGHT

Bullfrogs have a slimy covering on their skin to keep them cool and wet. Their skin has another special power. Bullfrogs can breathe through their skin! That helps them stay underwater for a long time.

Bullfrogs close their eyes when they swallow. Why? Their eyes sink down in their head and help push food down their throat. Weird!

tympanum

Bullfrog Body

A full-grown American bullfrog weighs about 1 pound (0.5 kg). Its hind legs are green or brown with spots. The legs are long and very strong, which helps the bullfrog jump. When jumping, a bullfrog's hind legs can **extend** to between 7 and 10 inches (18 and 25 cm) long. The legs fold behind the bullfrog's back when it's resting. The rest of an adult's body is 3 to 8 inches (8 to 20 cm) long.

FOOD FOR THOUGHT

Northern water snakes love to eat bullfrogs. When a bullfrog sees a predator like this snake or another bullfrog, it often sucks air into its body. This makes the bullfrog look bigger than it is. This could make the predator look for a smaller and easier meal.

Since bullfrogs tend to call loudly and are relatively small, they have many natural predators. Luckily, a bullfrog can jump up to 6 feet (1.8 m) when it senses a predator, such as a big fish or water snake.

Raccoons, herons, and largemouth bass hunt bullfrogs. When a bullfrog sees a predator, it jumps to escape.

The Great Pond Predator

Bullfrogs are usually nocturnal. This means they're mostly active at night, especially when it comes to hunting. When bullfrogs hunt, they hide and wait for prey. Their head is normally green or brown, which helps them blend in among plants near a pond or swamp's shore. Blending in to one's surroundings is also called camouflage.

FOOD FOR THOUGHT

Bullfrogs have webbed feet that help them swim fast and catch prey in the water.

When the bullfrog sees a tasty **insect**, it watches until the insect is close enough. Then, the bullfrog blasts off like a rocket! It jumps at the insect, opens its mouth, and sticks out its sticky tongue. It grabs the insect and gobbles it up!

A bullfrog's sticky tongue helps it grab its prey easily, especially bugs that are flying in the air. This bullfrog is chomping on a tasty worm.

15

A Hunter and a Cannibal

Bullfrogs eat a lot of insects, but insects are easy prey for these unstoppable hunters. Bullfrogs will also eat other frogs and even small snakes. They'll jump in the air to grab birds. They'll eat spiders, mice, turtles, and lizards. As long as the bullfrog can fit the prey in its mouth, it's dinnertime!

Bullfrog cannibalism is very common. Adult bullfrogs often eat young bullfrogs and tadpoles. Because they always have young bullfrogs around to eat, adult bullfrogs can survive and produce more young. That's why bullfrog populations can get out of control.

FOOD FOR THOUGHT

The bullfrog uses teeth on the roof of its mouth to grasp its prey. Then, the bullfrog swallows its prey alive and in one piece!

Scientists can study what's inside a bullfrog's stomach to see what they eat. The most common vertebrate found in a bullfrog's stomach is a smaller bullfrog.

Male bullfrogs are known for their loud croaking. When a bullfrog croaks, its throat puffs up like a balloon. Sometimes, the bullfrog is telling other male bullfrogs to stay away. Other times, he's trying to find a mate. The louder a male's call, the better! Some calls can be heard from about 0.5 mile (0.8 km) away. A female may choose a male with a louder call.

First, the female lays as many as 20,000 eggs in a lake or a pond. Then, the male **fertilizes** the eggs. Tadpoles break out of the eggs in about four days.

bullfrog eggs

female

Female bullfrogs croak, too. They don't croak as loudly as male bullfrogs, though, and humans can barely hear it.

FOOD FOR THOUGHT

You can tell the difference between male and female bullfrogs by the size of their tympana. A male's tympana are larger than its eyes, while a female's tympana are about the same size as its eyes. Also, females are slightly larger than males.

male

Life Cycle

When tadpoles break out of their eggs, they don't look like bullfrogs. Tadpoles look like tiny fish. They have fins and breathe through **gills**. They have a tail instead of legs.

Tadpoles eat plants, which makes them grow. They slowly change and grow legs. They grow lungs to breathe air, and their mouth and eyes get bigger. The tadpoles start to look more like frogs as time goes on. This change from a tadpole to a frog is called metamorphosis.

When tadpoles finally grow into bullfrogs, they're ready for the hunt. They might eat insects and small animals. They might even eat each other!

FOOD FOR THOUGHT

A bullfrog sheds its skin many times throughout its life. It opens its mouth and moves its body to loosen the old skin. The bullfrog pulls the skin over its head, then eats it!

In bullfrogs, metamorphosis takes about two years. In that time, there's a high risk that a tadpole or young frog will be eaten by a larger bullfrog. If they're lucky, bullfrogs can live up to seven years in the wild.

An Unstoppable Species

Humans brought bullfrogs into new places for food, which made the frogs an **invasive species**. Now, it's our duty to keep their numbers under control. Bullfrogs can put many habitats at risk because they tend to take over ponds and lakes. This leaves little food for native animals. Currently, there are many programs trying to track bullfrogs and decrease their populations. Luckily, bullfrog cannibalism helps keep populations down.

What makes bullfrogs so unstoppable? They eat anything, live in freshwater around the world, and if they can't find food, they'll gladly eat each other. These hungry cannibals are the kings of their freshwater homes.

Glossary

adapt: To change to fit new conditions.

cold-blooded: Having a body heat that changes with the surrounding heat.

extend: To make bigger or longer.

fertilize: To put male cells inside eggs to make babies.

gill: The body part a fish or tadpole uses to breathe underwater.

habitat: The natural home for plants, animals, and other living things.

insect: A small creature that has three body parts, six legs, and often has wings.

invasive species: Plants or animals that spread quickly in a new area and harm native plants and animals.

mate: One of two animals that come together to make babies.

membrane: A soft, thin layer of skin on an animal.

prey: An animal that is hunted by other animals for food.

species: A group of living things that are all the same kind.

Index

A
amphibians, 6
Asia, 8

C
call, 4, 13, 18

E
eggs, 18, 20
Europe, 8

F
females, 18, 19
freshwater, 4, 6, 9, 22

H
habitats, 4, 8, 22
hearing, 10

I
invasive species, 22

L
legs, 8, 12, 20

M
males, 18, 19
mate, 4, 10, 18
metamorphosis, 20, 21

N
North America, 4, 8

P
predators, 4, 10, 12, 13
prey, 10, 14, 15, 16

S
skin, 4, 9, 10, 21
South America, 8

T
tadpoles, 16, 18, 20, 21
teeth, 16
tongue, 15
tympana, 10, 11, 19

V
vision, 10

Y
young bullfrogs, 16, 21

Websites

Due to the changing nature of Internet links, PowerKids Press has developed an online list of websites related to the subject of this book. This site is updated regularly. Please use this link to access the list: www.powerkidslinks.com/ancan/frog